Fall
In the Gardens of Our Hearts

JENNIFER HORN

ISBN 978-1-68570-988-4 (paperback)
ISBN 978-1-68570-989-1 (digital)

Christian Faith Publishing
832 Park Avenue
Meadville, PA 16335
www.christianfaithpublishing.com

Printed in the United States of America

Introduction
Sitting in the Garden

He hath made every thing beautiful in his time:

—Ecclesiastes 3:11a (KJV)

God's marvelous, wonderous works can be seen in our outside earth and inside being. Just as each season holds fascinating details in variations of temperatures, scents, and sceneries throughout our earth world, so it is in the reflections of our internal heart world. We are individual in looks, personalities, and reactions. It was meant to be so by design of our Creator.

In view of all these changing seasons and patterns, we should take a moment to sit with our helper and teacher, the Holy Spirit, to look at what has emerged during the different seasons. Just as people travel to view the beautiful colors that seem to take over the landscapes in the fall, we too should view what has grown and is changing in our heart's gardens.

I pray and have hope that just as I discovered new life through my wonderful savior and friend Jesus Christ during a fall season, that you too will find the beauty of life with our Lord. He has created wonders in you, so sit with Him for a while in your heart's gardens with the help of this book in Jesus' name.

Jen Horn

CHAPTER 1

Come unto me, all ye that labour and are
heavy laden, and I will give you rest.

—Matthew 11:28 (KJV)

Plan to Know

Read 1 Corinthians 13:12 (MSG).

Key verse: "…We'll see it all then, see it all as clearly as God sees us, knowing him directly just as he knows us!" (1 Cor. 13:12b).

Fall season is a time to bring in harvests before winter arrives. Sometimes we will hesitate because we want all of what is growing to be picture perfect, both in the gardens of our heart and of our lives. The problem with that mindset is that we have not been perfect since the very first mistake and sin in the very first garden. God knowing this, still came to walk with us, talk with us, connect with us, and care for us. He loves us so much that He offered payment for the consequence of that decision for all of humanity so that we could reconnect to our original created purpose. We are created individual and unique and are wanted and loved. Loved so much that Christ died for that payment for us all.

During this fall season, instead of being hard on yourself for the imperfections you see coming up and out, look more closely for the growing beauty, the unique wonder, and grasp how deeply loved and cherished you are. Begin to know Him and connect to Him in that knowing. Watch as you spend time with Him how your life and the things inside of you become more clearly known.

Action Step

Discover Christ and His love for you when you read the Bible. Plan to read daily this fall season in the book of John. Start your mornings off by connecting more to God than before.

Prayer of Blessing

I bless you to connect to God and His love in your own individual way every day in Jesus' name. This is your original created purpose.

Prepare Your Heart

Read Psalms 10:16–18 (KJV).

Key verse: "…thou wilt prepare their heart, thou wilt cause thine ear to hear:" (Ps. 10:17b).

To think that the God of all creation and of all the universe would hear us and would listen to us. Wow, what a wonderful, marvelous thing.

Because this God created us different on purpose, how we speak, how we communicate, and how we connect is unique and individual to each of us. We each have a spot, our own place carved out just for us in God. We can reconnect through Christ to this place. We must choose to open our hearts and our lives to Him. We must prepare by making room and saying yes to God. In return, He hears and works in us, through us, and into our surrounding lives. Won't you open up and prepare for today's journey by spending time with Him and listening to Him speak to you through His Word?

Action Step

Humble yourself in what you want in everything by putting it second to the Lord's desire to reconnect and have a relationship with you. Christ paid for this because God wanted you and loves you. You must choose this first. He chooses you!

Prayer of Blessing

Holy Spirit of God, meet with the person reading this right now, where they are. Breathe Your life into every crevasse and help them reconnect in relationship today to the Lord Jesus Christ in Your name, Holy God.

Plant Hope

Read Job 11:18–19 (KJV).

Key verse: "And thou shalt be secure, because there is hope;" (Job 11:18a).

Do you find yourself believing God for everyone else but struggle to trust for yourself? Why do we do that? Insecurity, lack of confidence, fear? Here, we see that if we have hope then we can be secure because we trust.

Dare to believe that God can do for you, then believe that He will do it for you. You are His special creation in humanity. He loves you, and He likes you! Grab ahold of God's promises through Christ Jesus.

Action Step

Take a moment each day and meditate on the fact that God likes you and wants to be included with your day-to-day living.

Prayer of Blessing

I bless you to focus on the things that will remain throughout eternity, which is faith, hope, and love. May you be restored today in Jesus' name.

Plucking up Comparisons

Read Genesis 4:1–8 (KJV).

Key verse: "If thou doest well, shalt thou not be accepted?" (Gen. 4:7a).

In an age where you can see on the internet and media so many people's lives, it is easy to get your eyes off of your blessings in your unique individual life and begin to compare yourself to what you see portrayed by others. This seed of sin will grow up, and in the fall seasons of your life, produce harmful actions and words toward others.

In verse 4, it says that we must rule over this. How? By using the key of acceptance. Be pleased with who you are created by God to be; He is. Accept yourself and life in Christ; God does. Be thankful in who you are, in your relationship with the Lord, and in the path you are walking led by the Holy Spirit; He is with you. Be yourself and look to Christ as your model, not other fellow humans. Rule over sins of comparisons and live today content.

Action Step

Make a list of the goodness, blessings, and provisions in your life. Be thankful for them during this season. Everyday add to this list one more thing.

Prayer of Blessing

I bless you to see how uniquely wonderful you are. I bless you to do well today in looking to Christ and His Word as your focal point in Jesus' name.

Protecting Your Pathways

Read Matthew 3:16–4:1 (KJV).

Key verse: "Then was Jesus led up of the spirit…" (Matt. 4:1a).

After the supercharged growing season of summer, our yards, fields, and garden paths can be difficult to navigate due to the overgrowth. It is important to be able to see where you are walking to prevent injury. Adequate lighting to see while clearing your pathway can also reveal if there are any snakes, rocks, ticks, sticks, vines, debris, or other hazards. You must have these safe pathways around your growing areas so that the fall harvests can be brought in, and your gardens tended properly.

In Christ's kingdom, His example of the gift of the Holy Spirit brings a lighting direction (see verse 16). With this illumination and guidance of the way, Jesus was able to navigate the pathway. It was so important to Christ that we have this. He also instructs His disciples to wait for this gift. When the Holy Spirit gift arrived for the first disciples and illuminated them, it was like fire. Fire can give light to even the thickest darkest night. Once you receive this gift for yourself, you can follow the Spirit's lighted illumination in the day or night, knowing you can see your Spirit-protected pathways to step and work in safety.

Action Step

Read Acts chapters 1 and 2 in the Bible. Ask for and wait for your Holy Spirit gift and His illuminating protecting power.

Prayer of Blessing

I bless you to not take another step in your life today without being led by the Holy Spirit of God onto that step in Jesus' name.

Pruning Away Laziness

Read Proverbs 12:27–28 (MSG).

Key verse: "A lazy life is an empty life, but 'early to rise' gets the job done." (Prov. 12:27).

Fall season can bring the urge to just sit down and rest. Your body is tired from the summer extremes and workload. The garden is very lush with final harvests to be brought in. Shake yourself and get up after a small, very small, breathing rest pause. Do not be trapped in stopping now. Do not begin putting off what needs to be done now, today. The cold is coming soon.

In your walk with the Lord, you may also be tempted to over-extend rest periods. You may want to sleep for thirty minutes extra instead of getting up and connecting to God before your day begins. Prune away the urge of laziness or slothfulness as soon as it is noticed. If not pruned from your mind and actions, it will overtake your heart's garden and then over time will bring ruin, destruction, and separation from God one area at a time.

Action Step

After a day or two of rest, set your alarm once again to get up early to talk with, walk with, and connect to God in His Word and with worship.

Prayer of Blessing

I bless you to look up and see the bountiful harvest God has for you. I bless you to get up so you can take it in Jesus' name.

Producing Purpose

Read Genesis Chapters 2 and 3 (KJV).

Key verse: "And they heard the voice of the Lord God walking in the garden in the cool of the day:" (Gen. 3:8a).

Everything in the earth was created with creation systems set into motion. Such beauty, such wonder all around. Every day humanity connecting with God Himself. Imagine the walks and the talks about everything.

This is where we see the first mistake take place. Our curiosities used against us. Our desires lied to and deceived. Our choosing on our own without the walk, without the talk, without the connection to our loving God. Here we decide to choose outside of our created purpose. It caused loss of life connection and all that goes with that. But there is hope. God had a plan to restore us to that purpose through Christ. It is during a fall season that God showed up in my room, in my house, and whispered the hope of restoration into my heart. It is here that I told Him, "If you can do anything with this mess of my life, here, here it is." It is in this place that my created purpose was reconnected through the payment Christ paid for my sins, my mistakes, my deceptions. I gave up the self-choosing and started walking with God, listening and talking with God, connecting to Him in His Word. I began reading and listening to understand who He is so I could start to *be* who I was created to be. Won't you say yes to Him today and start producing who you were always purposed to *be*?

Action Step

Read the entire book of Luke in the Bible. Decide today to accept Christ's sacrifice of payment for you. Begin to connect daily with your God.

I bless you to see past every lie of the enemy trying to block you from knowing the Lord. I bless you with courage to say yes and with humility to follow His leading in Jesus' name.

CHAPTER 2

If I am so special to you, let me in on your plans.
That way, I will continue being special to you. Don't
forget, this is your people, your responsibility.

—Exodus 33:13 (MSG)

Plan to Write

Read Deuteronomy 4:39–40 (KJV).

Key verse: "Know therefore this day, and consider it in thine heart," (Deut. 4:39a).

Documenting your gardening successes and challenges is an important part of a fall season. It is by these notes, pictures, and dated entries that true evaluations can be made. If you have not been doing this, plan a time to complete this task so that you will be able to know what worked and what did not go so well.

I find that when I keep a journal of my life, thoughts, and experiences, I can look over the pages to see how things are progressing in my heart's gardens. It is good to know and consider these with the Lord so you can choose to receive the blessings in verse 40. Knowing that there is success, even in the smallest forms, will encourage you in the seasons to come.

Action Step

Plan a time to journal even just a sentence or two every day about what is happening, what you are thinking, feeling, and doing.

Prayer of Blessing

I bless you to face the truth and reality of everyday with the Lord. I bless you to read and write down God's promises about that with faith in Jesus' name.

Plan to Purchase

Read Matthew Chapter 25 (KJV).

Key verse: "But the wise took oil in their vessels with their lamps." (Matt. 25:4).

Fall season is a time to prepare for winter's approach by harvesting, preserving, and protecting plants. You must plan and make a purchase list of these things so you will have what is needed for the coming seasons. Many stores and sellers have extreme clearance markdowns on the items from the warmer months in order to make room for the winter holiday items. It is at this time you can stock up on items that you will use in the future. Be quick, these items do not stay long in stores selling at such good prices.

In the above scriptures, the wise took extra. They made a plan to get extra just in case needed. The foolish did not and had to go searching at a time they should have been ready. In the middle of the fall harvest, be sure to go get extra from the Lord's Presence. It is tempting to say that there is not enough time. You choose how you spend your days. Plan to get everything needed while it is available to you now.

Action Step

In the midst of the busyness, plan for a time on a Bible study of a topic from your heart's garden list. Make that study happen while you have it fresh in front of you before the winter holidays come.

Prayer of Blessing

I bless you to keep extra oil with you at all times in Jesus' name.

Plan to Overwinter

Read Psalm 27:4–5 (KJV).

Key verse: "For in the time of trouble he shall hide me in his pavilion:" (Ps. 27:5a).

Temperatures are changing. Now is the time for gardeners to plan how to overwinter their plants and trees. Will you cover them, wrap them, mulch them, or uproot them to bring into shelter? These things must be considered and planned for before the temperatures dip into freezing and before loss is incurred.

In your kingdom life, you must also take a moment to plan for what is coming. Do you want a solid, safe, protected place to survive life's cold harsh conditions that will come? Plan for time to be in God's protective Presence both individually daily and corporately with your Christ family weekly.

Action Step

Have you slacked off from your quiet times and church attendance? Plan to start again, so you can overwinter in protection the coming season.

Prayer of Blessing

I bless you to be aware of and feel the warm embrace of the Holy Spirit as you draw near to God individually and corporately in Jesus' name.

Plan to Compost

Read Proverbs 2:1–9 (KJV).

Key verse: "My son, if thou wilt receive my words, and hide my commandments with thee;" (Prov. 2:1).

Composting takes time to breakdown and become adequate nutrition that can readily be used by your plants. Fall is a great time to set this process up so that you have several months for it to sit and develop. There are different methods you can use depending on your space. I use a small worm bin where I can put scraps and small debris in. Within just a few short months, it is ready to go out into the garden.

Topical studies in the Bible can have similar effects. Take the topic of love for instance. By looking up the writings on love that the Bible contains and reading them, thinking on them, and then recording them in a journal can also, over time, become a condensed resource to then be added to your heart and life for healthy growth in the next season.

Action Step

Begin your Biblical composting accumulation by looking up scriptures with the words *charity* and *love*. Write them down in one place over the next three months to be ready for use in the winter months for the small things God will begin to start in you during that time.

Prayer of Blessing

I bless you to hide securely God's Word in your mind and heart in Jesus' name.

Plan to Plant Again

Read 2 Corinthians 9:6–8 (KJV).

Key verse: "But this I say, He which soweth sparingly shall reap also sparingly; and he which soweth bountifully shall reap also bountifully." (2 Cor. 9:6).

Fall is harvest time of crops previously sown. At the end of harvest, fatigue sets in and wanting to stop is a real thing. *Don't!* Take a day and plan time to plant again for the fall. There is another whole selection of plants that can stand cooler temperatures to give you much needed nourishment, fulfillment, and blessings. Plants like kale, turnips, beets, lettuce, greens, and peas.

Spiritually, take a moment and ask the Lord about planting again for more giving this season. There is still time. Let the Holy Spirit show you what to plant that will withstand the changes that are happening. In this extra planting, you will have an additional harvest for yourself and others this fall season.

Action Step

Take a day, today perhaps, to plan to plant again spiritually and naturally in your gardens. Write down your simple, easy-to-execute plan. Do this plan in the next week, don't wait!

Prayer of Blessing

I bless you to not stop this season but continue sowing and harvesting until the end in Jesus' name.

CHAPTER 3

Now get yourselves ready. I'm sending my Angel ahead of you to guard you in your travels, to lead you to the place that I've prepared.

—Exodus 23:20 (MSG)

Prepare to Get Knowledge

Read Psalm 119:64–68 (KJV).

Key verse: "Teach me good judgement and knowledge:" (Ps. 119:66a).

Fall is a great time to evaluate what went well and what you need to get more knowledge about for future success. I personally took gardening classes for several years and still listen to other gardeners as they teach what they know. There is so much information available now. You just need to prepare to go get it.

The same is true in the matters of the heart's gardens. There are classes, books, studies, and so much more available. Are you preparing yourself to be taught? Do you have a teachable mindset?

Action Step

Find one Bible study book that will help you have more knowledge in one area you would like to see more growth in. Set aside fifteen minutes a day to work your way through that study.

Prayer of Blessing

I bless you to receive from God's Word the knowledge to grow to full capacity in Jesus' name.

Prepare by Collecting Seeds

Read Psalm Chapter 126 (KJV).

Key verse: "He that goeth forth and weepeth, bearing precious seed, shall doubtless come again with rejoicing, bringing his sheaves with him." (Ps. 126:6).

Seed collecting from spent flowers, fruits, and vegetables is a great way to ensure your future plantings. The challenging part of this for myself is leaving the seeds to grow to full maturity before harvesting them to begin preparing them for storage. Time is necessary for this process to be successful. I find myself getting impatient and harvest them too soon. I am learning to wait.

In the above scripture, it shows that time, though challenging, can yield great results. Allow the Holy Spirit freedom of time constraints so that your seed can grow to not only produce a harvest in this season but also provide you with more seeds for future seasons.

Action Step

Prepare your mind by deciding not to harvest everything in your life too soon. Choose to trust God in His timing to guide you into full maturity.

Prayer of Blessing

I bless you to be led by the Holy Spirit in self-control so that there is joy in your season in Jesus' name.

Prepare by Cleansing

Read Psalms 19:7–14 (MSG).

Key verse: "…Then I can start this day sun-washed, scrubbed clean of the grime of sin." (Ps. 19:13b).

As the growing season comes to an end in the fall, a gardener will begin to prepare equipment by cleaning them. One by one, as they are used for their final time, they will be cleaned, put aside, and stored for the next season.

Here in these verses, we see the importance of having our lives, minds, and hearts scrubbed clean. The scripture reading tells us how this is done. Make sure to prepare for use in the coming growing season by cleansing this fall.

Action Step

Reread verses 7–9. Begin to clean up the places in you and your life that have no respect or reverence for God. You can check these places to see how clean they are by comparing them to the reflections of the laws, commandments, statutes, and judgements found in the Bible.

Prayer of Blessing

I bless you to not store thoughts, attitudes, and mindsets away without cleansing them with the Word of God in Jesus' name.

Prepare for First Frost

Read Proverbs 6:6–11 (MSG).

Key verse: "…at harvest it stockpiles provisions." (Prov. 6:8b).

Whatever you planted in your garden is ready weekly (sometimes daily) for harvest and preserving. If you do not make time to process these things before the first frost, you can miss the abundant blessings of your garden.

So it is in the spiritual kingdom. There is no time for laying down. Press into your connection with God and let the Holy Spirit help you with strength and wisdom of timing. Everything is ready to be gathered and preserved for yourself and gifted to others. Do not let your blessings be curses and wasted. Prepare to harvest now before the cold comes.

Action Step

Take a lesson from the ant which goes out daily and brings something in for the day and future. Ask the Holy Spirit every morning to help you with today's gatherings.

Prayer of Blessing

I bless you to not be anxious about the overwhelming amount of harvest. I bless you to step by step, hour by hour, to walk with the Lord in today's gardening of your heart adventure in Jesus' name.

CHAPTER 4

Thou shalt bring them in, and plant them in the
mountain of thine inheritance, in the place, O Lord,
which thou hast made for thee to dwell in, in the
Sanctuary, O Lord which thy hands have established.

—Exodus 15:17 (KJV)

Plant Bulbs

Read Proverbs 20:4 (KJV).

Key verse: "The sluggard will not plow by reason of the cold; therefore shall he beg in harvest, and have nothing." (Prov. 20:4).

There are bulbs like garlic and tulips that do well and actually thrive when planted just before frost. Just because the temperatures are cooling, does not mean the planting season has ended.

The same is true in the Christ kingdom. Ephesians 5:9 talks about how all the spirit fruit is incased in goodness. The bulb casings in the natural absorb and protect the plantings inside just like goodness protects the Spirit fruit inside. So plant your bulbs of goodness in every area of your heart, mind, and life.

Action Step

Look up scriptures that contain the word *goodness*. Write them down for memorizing to encase your planting efforts this fall in your life's gardens.

Prayer of Blessing

I bless you to be aware you are encased with God's goodness in Jesus' name.

Plant Trees and Shrubs

Read Ephesians 5:19–33 (KJV).

Key verse: "Giving thanks always for all things unto God and the Father in the name of our Lord Jesus Christ;" (Eph. 5:20).

Planting trees and shrubs in early fall so they have some time to get established before cold temperatures is something gardeners consider. Once the freezing temperatures set in, it is considered too late. By doing this early in the season, birds, squirrels, and other creatures also have time to get prepared in the branches so they too can survive the cold coming.

In the Christ kingdom, you can also create an environment in your home for children to be protected from the harsh conditions that will come. A husband must plant in love. A wife plants in respect. These planted within the homes give a place for the children to grow and be protected. Although planting takes work, you can give thanks to God every day in everything knowing He will walk with you and help these become established.

Action Step

Husbands look up scriptures containing the word *love*. Wives look up scriptures in the Bible that contain the word *respect*. Everyone, unmarried and married, look up scriptures that contain *giving thanks* and write them down. Practice planting action for winter is coming so prepare now.

Prayer of Blessing

I thank my Lord Jesus Christ for you all. Amen.

Plant by Division

Read John 7:37–43 (KJV).

Key verse: "So there was a division among the people because of him." (John 7:43).

A gardener that wants to save money and a trip to the local nursery or box store will divide perennials. They can be planted in the same area or in an entirely different area of the garden. Fall is a great time to do this before they go dormant.

In the scripture reading today, we find that there was a division in the people due to what Jesus had spoken. Some believed, some questioned, some doubted entirely. If they would have known the scriptures, they would have realized that this was the very promised Christ and allowed the questions to bring more truth in the division. Are you having doubts and questions about Jesus? Allow the Holy Spirit to reveal the Bible's truth into those areas so you will get more for planting.

Action Step

Write down in your journal every area you have doubts, questions, and divisions in. Ask the Holy Spirit to guide you as you search out the answers in the Bible.

Prayer of Blessing

I bless you to not run away from division questions but rather face them head on. May the Holy Spirit bring peace and unity in your heart and mind in Jesus' name.

Plant Cover Crops

Read Numbers 9:15–17 (KJV).

Key verse: "So it was alway: the cloud covered it by day," (Num. 9:16a).

Cover crop planting helps the soil to not erode away. It can also add to the soil value when tilled under before the spring plantings. Gardeners see the value in protecting the soil even when lying dormant for a season.

In the above scriptures, we see that God's glory covers and directs. You can protect your heart's garden soil and add more value to it by being in God's Presence. Plant moments of worship into your life. Let God cover you so nothing of value will be lost even in your dormant season.

Action Step

Attend church regularly for corporate worship. Set aside space and time in your daily life to worship the living God.

Prayer of Blessing

I bless you to crave God connection through worship in Jesus' name.

CHAPTER 5

A time to be born, and a time to die; a time to plant,
and a time to pluck up that which is planted;

—Ecclesiastes 3:2 (KJV)

Pluck up Problems

Read Luke 17:1–10 (MSG).

Key verse: "…If you have a bare kernel of faith, say the size of a poppy seed, you could say to this sycamore tree, 'Go jump in the Lake,' and it would do it." (Luke 17:6b).

Fall garden chores can include plucking up dead or dying plants. You need to pick up all fallen fruit. You must weed control by pulling up, spraying, and covering to smother out any chance of growth or regrowth from seeds. If any of these things are left in the garden, it can cause problems for seasons to come.

Kingdom life can have similar fall chores also. In this scripture passage, we need to pluck up offenses, unforgiveness, and self-entitlement. How can one do this? By speaking to them and casting them out of your heart, mind, and life. Confess these sins so that in faith they can be plucked up and removed from your heart's gardens.

Action Step

Write down 1 John 1:9 in your journal. Write out your faith confessions to God. Begin to serve others where God has helped you.

Prayer of Blessing

I bless you to use the faith God has given you today in Jesus' name.

CHAPTER 6

Keep me as the apple of the eye, hide me
under the shadow of thy wings,

—Psalm 17:8 (KJV)

Protect from Cold

Read Psalm 27:4–6 (KJV).

Key verse: "For in the time of trouble he shall hide me in his pavilion: in the secret of his tabernacle shall he hide me;" (Ps. 27:5a).

Fall is a time to take action to protect against the temperatures that will kill garden plants and trees. Some ways a gardener may do this is mulching, covering, and wrapping the plants. Sometimes a gardener will even dig up to set plants indoors for protection. If not done during the fall season while temperatures are still above freezing, you can sustain loss.

Such it is in the spiritual kingdom. God will hide and protect you from trouble as the above scriptures say. Do you have God's secret place location? In these scriptures it says that He is in His dwelling place. Because the Holy Spirit lives in you and gives access through Christ due to His payment for us, we can go into the connecting private spot God has just for each of us. Won't you draw near to Him? He is waiting closer than you know.

Action Step

Put on some worship music and gather yourself into a private spot and allow God to surround you today.

Prayer of Blessing

I bless you to know the Holy God in Jesus' name. He loves you. He is near you.

CHAPTER 7

...the chastisement of our peace was upon him;
and with his stripes we are healed.

—Isaiah 53:5b (KJV)

Prune to Shape

Read Proverbs 3:11–12 (KJV).

Key verse: "My son, despise not the chastening of the Lord; neither be weary of his correction:" (Prov. 3:11).

Fall garden pruning includes deadheading spent flowers and slight shaping cuts of branches. This enhancing and solidifying the shaping before the plant goes dormant in the cooling temperatures will keep them looking nice throughout the season.

The Father is our heart's garden pruner. He will orchestrate the removal of old mindsets and actions. He will shape you in love. You are His children. Never hate His shaping even when hard and hurtful. His timing is perfect as are His ways of doing things. He sees the full picture of how things should be and turn out. You can trust Him.

Action Step

Evaluate the areas where you feel God is shaping. Work with Him in these areas by not running away from Him and His Word.

Prayer of Blessing

I bless you to let old actions, habits, and mindsets go before the cross of Christ in Jesus' name.

CHAPTER 8

But the river itself, on both banks, will grow fruit trees of all kinds. Their leaves won't wither, the fruit won't fail. Every month they'll bear fresh fruit because the river from the Sanctuary flows to them. Their fruit will be for food and their leaves for healing.

—Ezekiel 47:12 (MSG)

Produce Life

Read Deuteronomy 30:16–20 (KJV).

Key verse: "…therefore choose life, that both thou and thy seed may live:" (Deut. 30:19b).

Everything planted this year hopefully grew and produced. For the gardener, fall is the time to harvest before the cold sets in with winter. It is an exciting time if what was planted was good and cared for. The weeds and buggy fungus plants, they were not a blessing. It is here, during the fall seasons that what I had worked on truly was revealed. My efforts put to tangible results. Am I pleased with those results?

It is also during a fall season where my internal life revealed a lot of bad seed results. I was given this scripture choice. I could choose new life and its blessing promises or death seeds with cursings. Truthfully, I was reaping the latter already. As I considered and fought against God's love, the reality of the truth of my life played over and over in my thoughts. I felt that I did not deserve Christ's payment to reconnect with God, and I told Him so. I gave excuses of my current emotional state, my life's failures, and my fleshly addictions. The Lord spoke a simple statement into my mind and heart by saying if I would just give myself and my life to Him as it was, then He would take care of the rest. I believed Him, and it was that fall night many years ago that I chose life with God. God has held true to His promise. Every day, I choose to walk with Him, to talk with Him, and to connect with Him. Written in the pages of this book series of seasons are small reflections of that connection.

Action Step

Take a moment right now to consider today life or death seeds. You choose!

Prayer of Blessing

I bless you to overstep every obstacle and excuse so you can be connected/reconnected with God today in Jesus' name.

Producing Love

Read 2 John 1:4–6 (MSG).

Key verse: "Love means following his commandments, and his unifying commandment is that you conduct your lives in love. This is the first thing you heard, and nothing has changed." (2 John 1:6).

How is your harvesting going? Are you having an overflow of abundance? Is it all that you had imagined it would be? Your soil health was the root of whether the harvest is successful in producing your produce. The testing if your soil was adequate or not was proven over the growing seasons by the harvests.

Your heart soil also will be tested over the growing seasons. Fall spiritual kingdom seasons will give you your tests and the results by the fruit of how you spoke and acted toward God, yourself, and others. What were the tests exactly? Hebrews 5:8 (MSG) says, "Though he was God's son, he learned trusting-obedience by what he suffered, just as we do." Trusting God and following His commandments when the hard times come, when the sufferings happen, is the test. Over the growing seasons of life when things were hard, tiring, and you hurt with sufferings having to "push" through, did you love God, yourself, and others the way God says to in 1 Corinthians 13? The harvest of your words and actions will reveal how much of this fruit you really produced this growing season. It will also reveal the health of your internal heart soil. God is love. If you need more for the next growing season in your soil so you can produce outward fruit also, get more of Him.

Action Step

There are three things according to 1 Corinthians 13 that last in you into eternity. Love/charity is one of them and the best one. Set it at the top every day to get more of God who is love. Do this by connecting to Him in reading His written words to you, communicating with Him in prayer, and letting Him be present with you in worship.

Prayer of Blessing

I bless you to produce abundant love fruit with the help of the Holy Spirit and to evaluate your true harvest of it by how you respond outwardly when sufferings of life happen. Be fruitful in Jesus' name.

Producing Hope

Read Romans 5:3–5 (KJV).

Key verse: "And not only so, but we glory in tribulations also: knowing that tribulation worketh patience; And patience, experience; and experience, hope:" (Rom. 5:3–4).

Are you having a wonderful fall harvest season? Are you able to have feelings of accomplishment in the experience you have acquired over the growing seasons? Do you now have more hope with excitement over the possibilities by applying all that you have learned to the next seasons? Your harvests will prove your experience in gardening. Remember that your unique location, extreme weather conditions, and varieties of personally selected plants, bushes, and trees, all factor into your final outcomes. Patience and consistent working efforts during the trials and tribulations of each season will give you proven experience of what works and what does not. With that knowledge, you will find hope of more harvests for yourself and for others in the seasons to come.

I would like to have internal hope without the tribulations, the harsh conditions, the consistent effort day in and day out regardless of how I feel. Just like the gardener, I must consistently work long term through the conditions and seasons of life. The Holy Spirit will give the security of the love of God being with us so that we have strength to keep going. It is only from going through the process in the above scriptures that we can produce more hope. This is also one of the things we take into eternity with us according to 1 Corinthians 13. Make this #2 on your must-have fruits to produce and harvest.

Action Step

Choose to focus on God and His perspective when the hard things happen. Ask the Holy Spirit to give wisdom like in James 1:5

for your unique set of circumstances. Choose today to keep going day in and day out with God no matter what.

Prayer of Blessing

I bless you to not be sideswiped by the lies of the enemy that says that what you are going through is impossible. Know all things are possible through Christ Jesus by staying connected to the living God. I bless you with supernatural, Holy Ghost infused strength to breathe and stand in that connection today in Jesus' name.

Producing Faith

Read Hebrews 11:1 (KJV).

Key verse: "NOW faith is the substance of things hoped for, the evidence of things not seen." (Heb. 11:1).

I have a question for you that you must answer to yourself honestly. Is what you are seeing in your harvests during this fall season the very thing that you saw in your dreams of these days in the beginning? I took classes at my local library and would watch videos of gardeners working their gardens and bringing in their harvests while I was learning all about this new hobby. When it came time to really plan for my personal garden, I found myself leaning on the possibilities and hoping that I would have successes also. I believed that if I followed the information, working like they did, and applying it to my unique location, that I too would experience harvests. And I did!

In the spiritual kingdom, faith is the first thing listed in 1 Corinthians 13:13 of the three things that will abide forever. How do we get more of it so we can produce more? Romans 10:17 (KJV) says, "So then faith cometh by hearing, and hearing by the word of God." This hearing is not just a mere listening, but a listening with understanding, and that comes by the utterance/words of God. I had to choose to search out gardeners that spoke in such a way that I could understand what they were saying and instructing. I do not have to search so hard in the spiritual kingdom. We only need the gift Jesus sent in the Holy Ghost. John 14:26 says, "But the Comforter, which is the Holy Ghost, whom the Father will send in my name, he shall teach you all things, and bring all things to your remembrance, whatsoever I have said unto you." Because God made us, He sent us the Holy Spirit to speak like we learn into our hearts. He will guide us through the lessons in the Bible, helping our understanding so we can apply it to our unique situations. It is here, listening/hearing God's possibilities and successes, that if we follow the information, living out the examples that we can picture in faith that we also will have those outcomes. Do you have the Holy Spirit teacher guiding you?

Action Step

Christ has paid for and given us all we need to plant, produce, and harvest *all* of the spiritual kingdom fruit even the ones that will last eternal. Decide to listen to the Holy Spirit, and do what He helps you to understand to do in the lessons of the Words of God. Believe in faith that God's connection, promises, and fruit are for you!

Prayer of Blessing

I bless you to trust for all that God has for you now and for eternity in Christ Jesus' name. Amen.

Producing Peace

Read Philippians 4:6–9 (KJV).

Key verse: "And the peace of God, which passeth all understanding, shall keep your hearts and minds through Christ Jesus." (Phil. 4:7).

Did you talk to God about your external and internal gardens? I enjoy in the fall walking around and appreciating the beauty and wonders of the garden and all it has brought for the year. I find myself telling the Lord how wonderful I think He is to have given me the opportunity to have a garden and to watch it produce with His creative power. These verses also say that thankfulness should have a part also in our communication.

During the fall season, my family takes time to remember all the wonderful things God has done. We are thankful to be with Him and with each other. We are thankful for the blessings He has brought to us. We set aside time to get together and share food and conversation with each other about how everything has been going. We pray together over a wonderful meal. I like thanking God for His abundance and provision. Giving God all of your requests and then offering up to Him gratitude will dissolve away worry and anxiety. In their place, peace is produced. Choose the way of peace today.

Action Step

For every worry request, think of three things that you are thankful for also. Tell God everything that you have considered.

Prayer of Blessing

I bless you to follow the way of producing peace in Jesus the Prince of Peace's name.

Producing Rest

Read Genesis 2:1–3 (KJV).

Key verse: "And God blessed the seventh day, and sanctified it: because that in it he had rested from all his work which God created and made." (Gen. 2:3).

The garden season is coming to a close, and it is time to put the garden beds to rest. At this time, some gardeners choose to add compost and some do not. This is a preference for you to decide. This is one of the last of the garden chores at the end of the harvest in the fall. The gardener can now enjoy some rest.

God set aside a day to rest after His work of creation. He blessed that rest time. We can choose to not feel guilty or stressed for taking rest. The outside gardens and seasons reflect a time to rest. Enjoy and rejuvenate from the outside and inside garden work. Be blessed today in your resting.

Action Step

Plan to take time to rest. Put it on your calendar and then do it.

Prayer of Blessing

I bless you in your time of rest to walk with God, talk with God, and enjoy resting with your wonderful Creator in Jesus' name.

About the Author

Jennifer Horn currently resides in Florida. She enjoys life as a wife, mother, and grandmother all while working in a salon as an independent stylist. Her hobby of gardening started out as a way to manage stress and over time has become so much more.